Painting The Darkness **Brighter**

By Zachary Burres

This chapbook is dedicated to all my new internet friends. I'm constantly blown away by how much love and support there is out there in our little community for poetry like this. I hope this collection of short poems paints your day a little brighter. Thanks for reading!

Look Up

Worried artist
Please look up
You are surrounded
By your own brilliance
That you barely
Ever notice

2

Brilliantly

If the world is falling apart
Outside
Focus on your garden
Inside
And when the world is ready again
So shall you be
To shine, shine, shine
Brilliantly

Brighter

There is a day
When the broken poet realizes
His power
Is in painting the darkness brighter

All I Need to Be

I suck at a lot of things
Most of them, actually
I can't fix a car
Or keep a lover
And I tend to overthink
But damn it, that's my strong-suit
A dreamer
That's all I need to be

Sad Song

The universe is music

And sometimes it's a sad song

But sometimes

That's the one we needed to hear

A Secret

I'll tell you a secret
Young creative
If you want to really make it
Show them when they're naked
That they aren't as fragile as they thought

Flaws

You're the only one
Who sees your flaws so intimately
And none of them are permanent

Chin Up

Chin up
Because right now
Your past self is jealous
And your future self is proud

Overthinking

I've been overthinking
That what if this curse is a blessing
If the gears are always turning
Anyway
If the stream is always flowing
Why not tap in
And channel it
Into something beautiful?

Empty Space

There's no empty space
That the creative heart can't fill

Soon

At first you'll probably suck
But soon
You'll be picking the stars out of the sky
Without even getting out of your chair

If You Became Grateful

To those who have much
And to those who have little
We know what happens to each of them
But regardless of what you currently are
If you became grateful
Which would you be then?

Heaven & Hell

Heaven and Hell aren't places
They're perspectives

Permission & Regret

You'll probably
Regret something anyway
It's better if you take that
As permission to be yourself

Too Loud

The thoughts in your head
May be too loud
Because they're not being drowned out
By the sound of your footsteps

That busted old piano
Broken keys
And almost no tuning
But
It still makes music

First Question

This is beautiful!
Is the first thought
But
How could it be better?
Is the first question
Of an artist

The Edge

Don't feel scared for dancing
Along the abyss's rugged edge
You've done this your whole life
Without ever falling in

Cracks In The World

Goodbye
Did not destroy the world
It only cracked it
But from the fissures
I see a glorious light
Harvesting that
Should keep me sane

Start Small

They'll all giggle
But you have to start now
Because big things
Only ever come
From small ones

Better Than Expected

Slumped into my chair
Coffee beside
Prepared
To finally get something done
But
What does it all add up to?
I'll check first
Because I must know
Oh--
It's actually working

The War

There will always be pain
Inside the trenches
But my darling
You're winning the war

Obstacles

Mountains?
No matter,
I will move them
Rivers?
Not a problem,
I will drink them
Caverns?
Filled with creatures?
I will defeat them all
Doubt?
Sometimes, until I remember
Everything I have so far overcome

Reframe

Your patterns need not be prisons
They can be runways instead
Your memories need not be painful
They can be lessons instead
Just enough can be plenty
If you let it

Play It Loud

The ones who want to listen
Will stay
The ones who hates the noise
Will leave
So play it loud
And the ones meant to find you
Will

My brain is whirling to know
How to focus
How to get this thing over with
I guess
I chose this
But
Now I have to follow through with it?
Maybe I'm useless
But
Maybe I won't let that be true

If You Would Just

The world doesn't need
To be upon your shoulders
It could instead
Be between your hands
If you would just
Create

Flammable

The soul
Is the most flammable material
Sometimes
It takes only a word
Of encouragement

Thanks

Before you log off
To be a million miles away again
Thanks
For making this lonely world
A little easier to be in

www.ingramcontent.com/pod-product-compliance
Lightning Source LLC
Chambersburg PA
CBHW071504150726
48000CB00006B/2686